ABC
of the Human Body

table of contents

Arteries

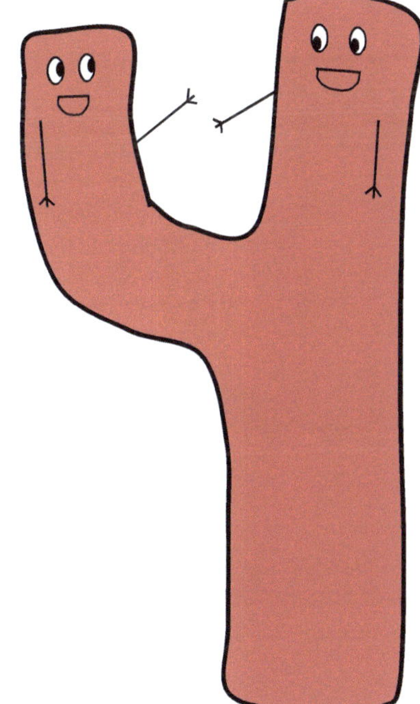

What is an artery?

Arteries are blood vessels that carry oxygenated blood and nutrients from the heart to the lungs and tissues

What do they look like?

Individually, arteries are thick tubes composed of muscle. The inside is covered with smooth tissue. There are a total of three layers; the intima, media, and adventitia.

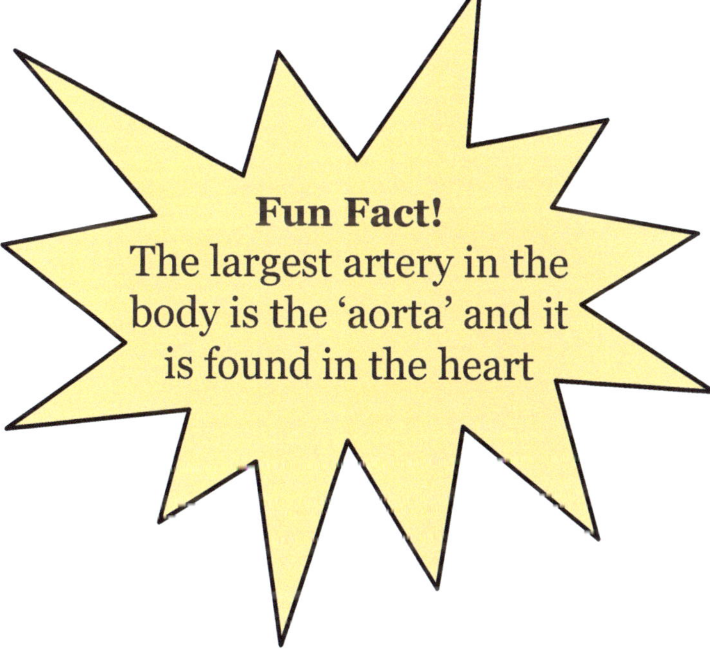

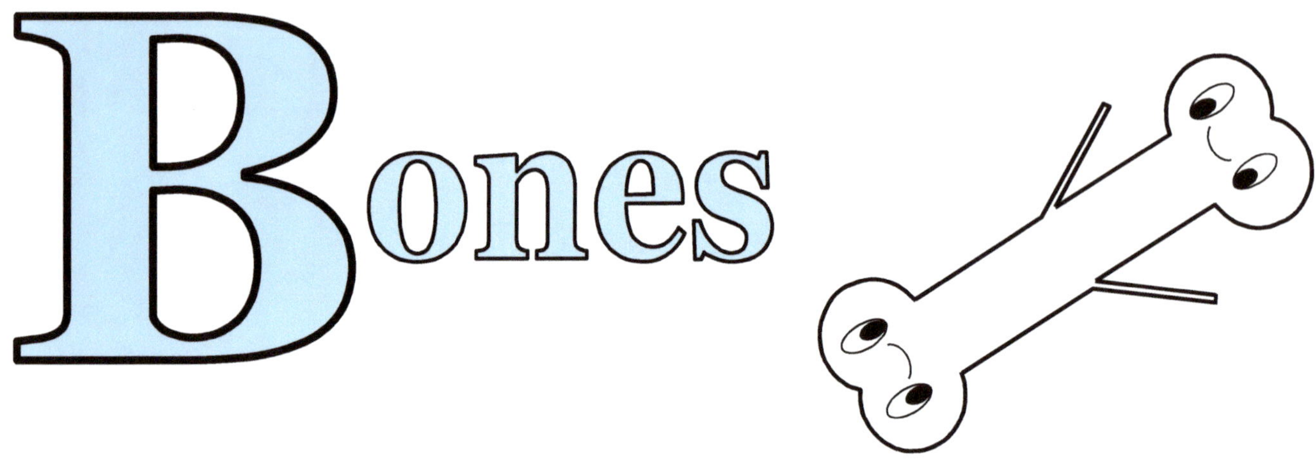Bones

What is a bone?

Bones are hardened, calcified tissue that make up the skeleton- the main structural component of the body

How many types are there?

There are five different types of bones; the long bones, the short bones, the flat bones, the irregular bones, and the sesamoid bones

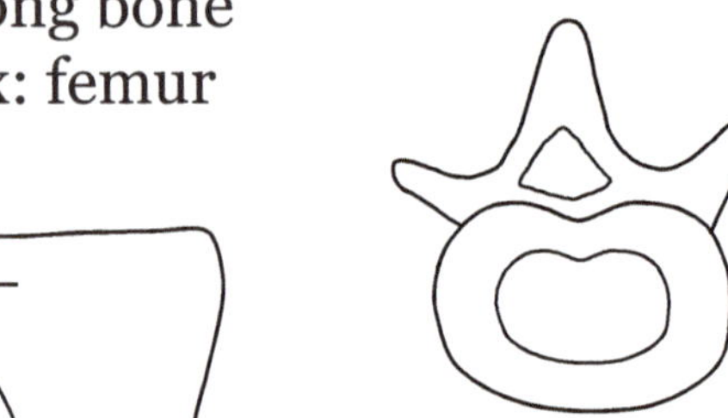

Short bone
Ex: carpals

Long bone
Ex: femur

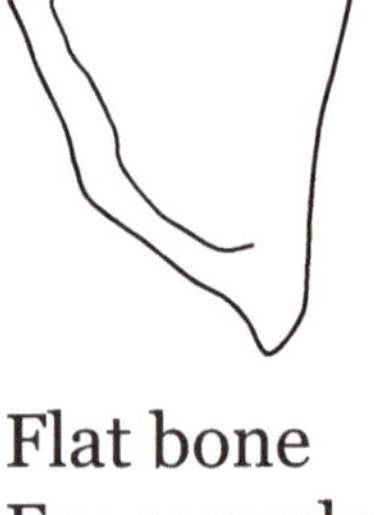

Irregular bone
Ex: vertebra

Flat bone
Ex: scapula

Sesamoid bone
Ex: patella

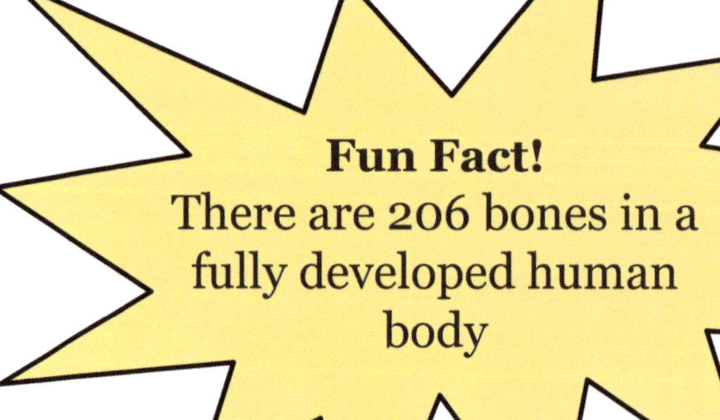

Cells

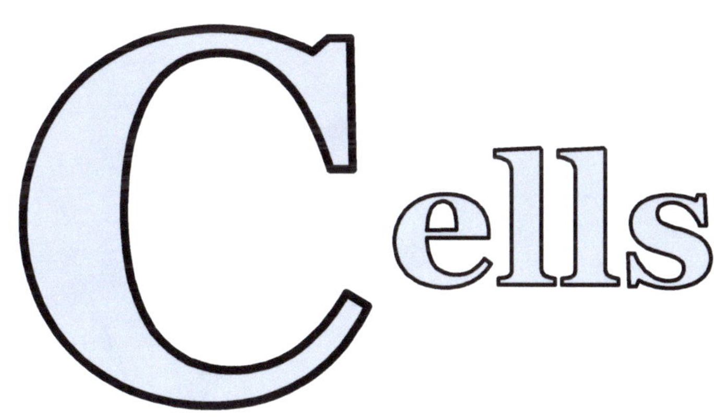

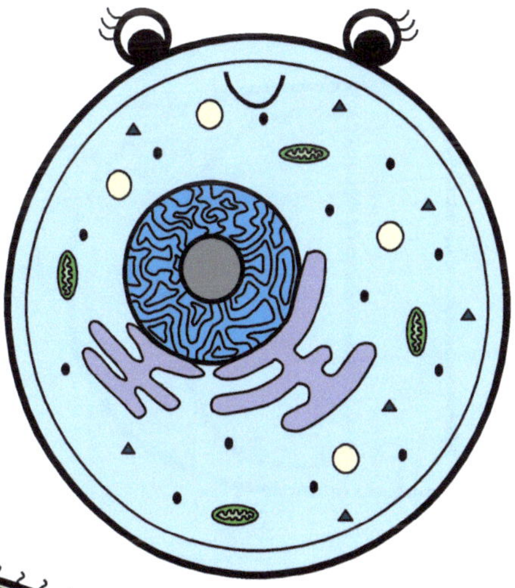

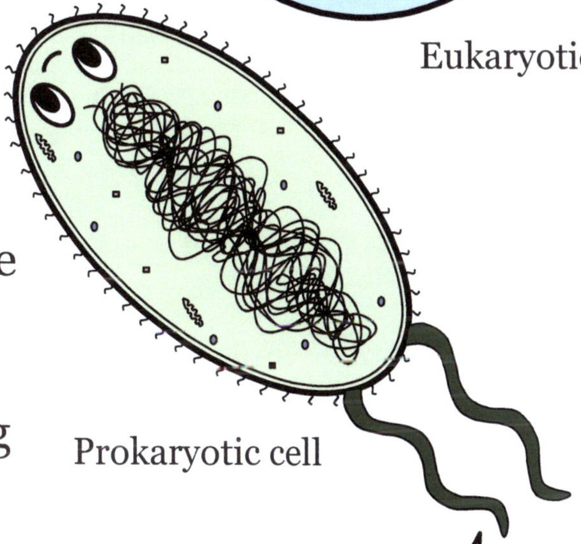

Eukaryotic cell

Prokaryotic cell

What is a cell?

Cells are the smallest unit of life that can live independently. Inside cells are organelles which power the cells much like organ systems power the body. Every living thing is made up of cells

What are the different cells?

There are two main classifications; eukaryotic cells and prokaryotic cells. Eukaryotic cells have a nucleus and mainly must be in multicellular environments to survive. Prokaryotic cells do not have a defined nucleus and can survive as unicellular organisms.

Fun Fact!
Bacteria, a kind of prokaryotc, was the first life forms found on Earth.

D^{NA}

(deoxyribonucleic acid)

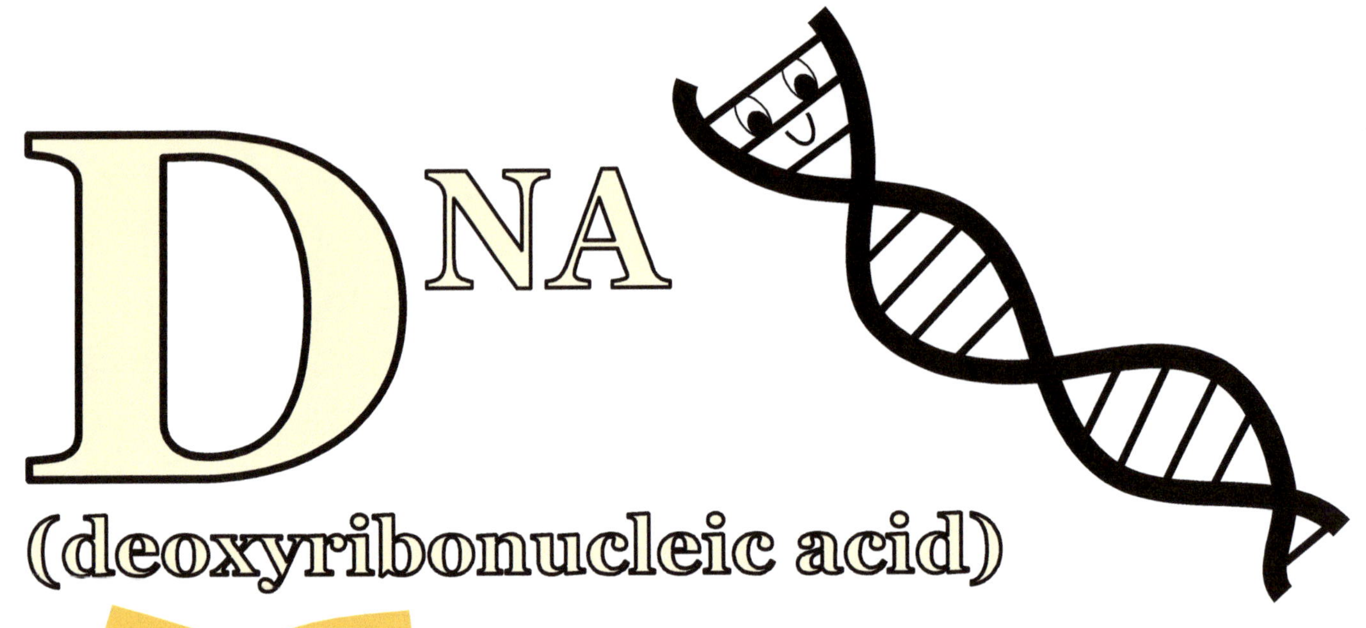

What is a DNA?

DNA is a genetic instruction manual located in the nucleus of a cell that is responsible for developing each aspect of an organism's being. Half of your DNA comes from your mother and the other half comes from your father

How does DNA work?

DNA is packaged and wrapped into coils to create chromosomes. The chromosomes that don't determine gender are called autosomes and humans have 22 pairs of those (so 44 total).

Fun Fact!
DNA consists of four bases: adenine, thymine, cytosine, and guanine.

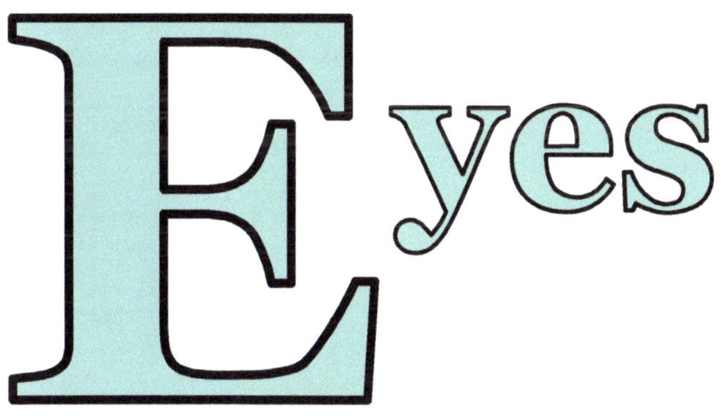Eyes 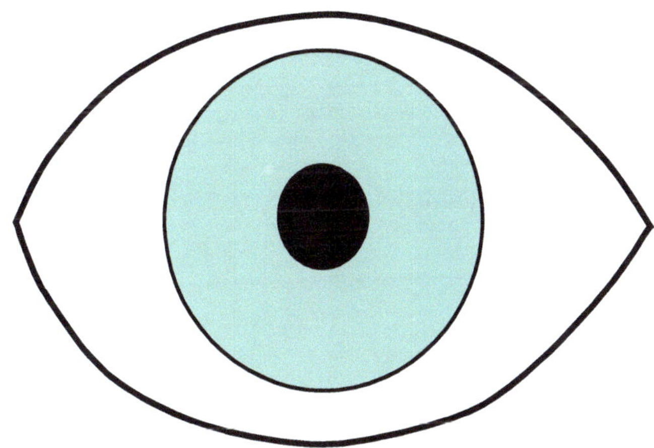

What is the eye?

The eye is an organ that is used for seeing which is your sense of vision. In humans, the primary parts are the iris, cornea, lens, vitreous humor, retina, pupil, aqueous humor, and optic nerve. Light enters via the cornea and travels through the eye until it reaches the optic nerve. The optic nerve sends the information to the brain resulting in sight.

How is color perceived?

The eye contains two types of photoreceptors* for seeing: rod cells and cone cells. Rods help you see in bad/dim lighting and cones help you see in regular/well lit areas. The cones are the cells that perceive color.

*Photoreceptors: cells in the eye that capture light.

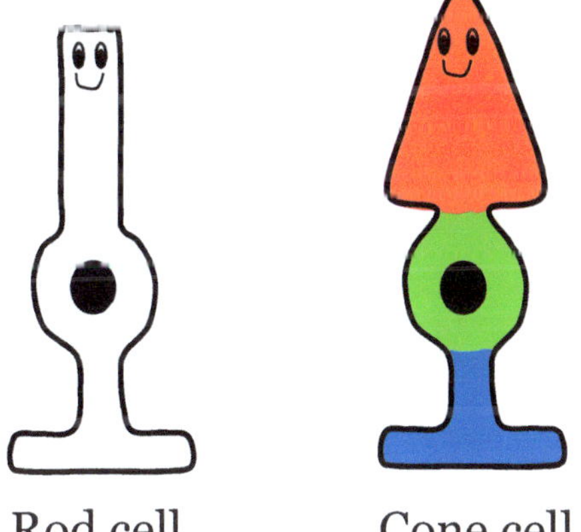

Rod cell   Cone cell

Fingers

What are fingers?

Fingers are the limbs that hang off the tips of your hand. Typically, humans have five of them. They are used to help us perform fine movements such as writing, picking things up, playing an instrument, etc.

Why are fingers so sensitive?

Each human fingertip contains 3,000+ touch receptors making it one of the most sensitive parts of the body. Because the surface area of our fingertips are so small, these touch receptors overlap, amplifying the sensitivity.

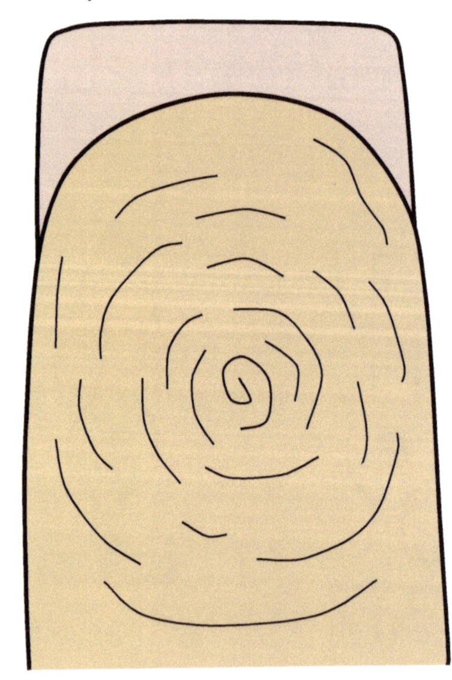

 Gallbladder

What is the gallbladder?

The gallbladder is a small organ that resides under the liver and is seemingly resembles a pear. It contains bile which is released after consuming meals.

What is bile?

Bile is a greenish-brownish fluid stored in the gallbladder that assists with the decomposition of fats. It also redirects waste which is why feces is the color it is.

Heart

What is the heart?

The heart is the main organ of the circulatory system as it pumps blood to the entire body. It is made up of three types of cardiac tissue: the endocardium which is the innermost layer, the myocardium which is the middle layer, and the epicardium which is the outermost layer.

What are the sections of the heart?

The heart consists of four chambers: the right ventricle, the right atrium, the left ventricle and the left atrium. The right side of the heart pumps deoxygenated blood to the lungs and the left side of the heart receives oxygenated blood that is then distributed to the test of the body

Intestines

Large intestine

<u>What is the small intestine?</u>

The small intestine is the first part of the intestinal tract. The semi-digested food and stomach acid fluid (chyme) move down to the first part of the small intestine which is the duodenum. Then it travels down to the second part, the jejunum, and lastly the ileum. In these parts, the nutrients are absorbed from the chyme.

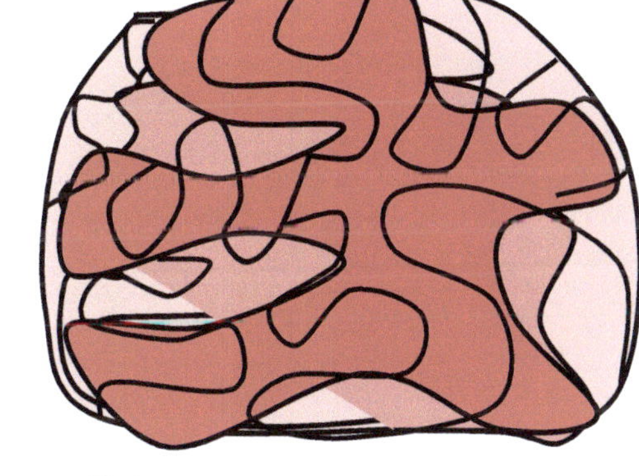

Small intestine

<u>What is the large intestine?</u>

Otherwise known as the colon, the large intestine is the last part of the digestive system before the feces is excreted. Water is absorbed from the leftover chyme exiting the small intestine and the rest is to be pushed out of the anus.

Joints

What is a joint?

A joint is the meeting point of two (sometimes more) bones to allow mobility. Different types of joints include saddle, hinge, ball and socket, gliding, condyloid, and hinge.

What does it mean to be double jointed?

When the name is literally broken down, it means that there are two joints in the place of one. This, however, is incorrect as it is not possible. What it really means is that the joint can move past what is viewed as typical mobility range.

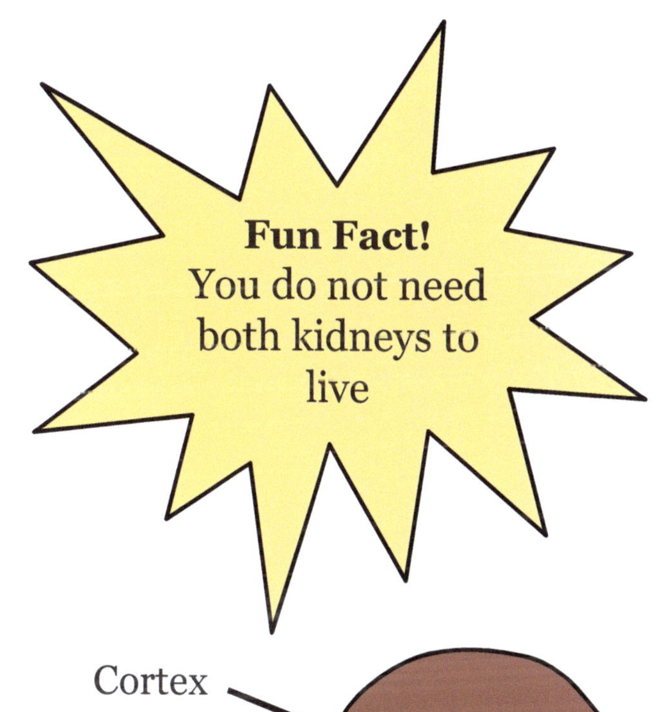Kidneys

What are kidneys?

Kidneys are organs that mainly function to take excess fluid waste from the body and turn it into urine. It also filters the blood to get rid of all toxins. They also resemble beans.

How do kidneys filter?

Each kidney uses filtering units known as nephrons. There are about one million nephrons per kidney. There are two parts to the nephron filtering process; the glomerulus and the tubule. The glomerulus filters the blood while the tubule takes the important components of the blood and returns them back plus, making urine.

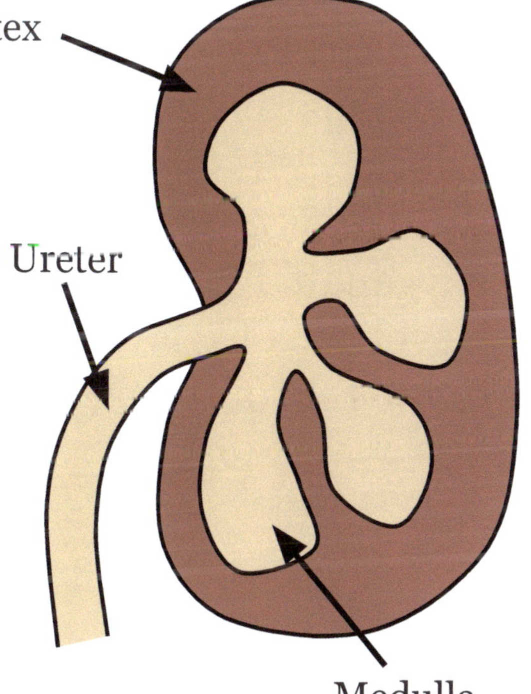

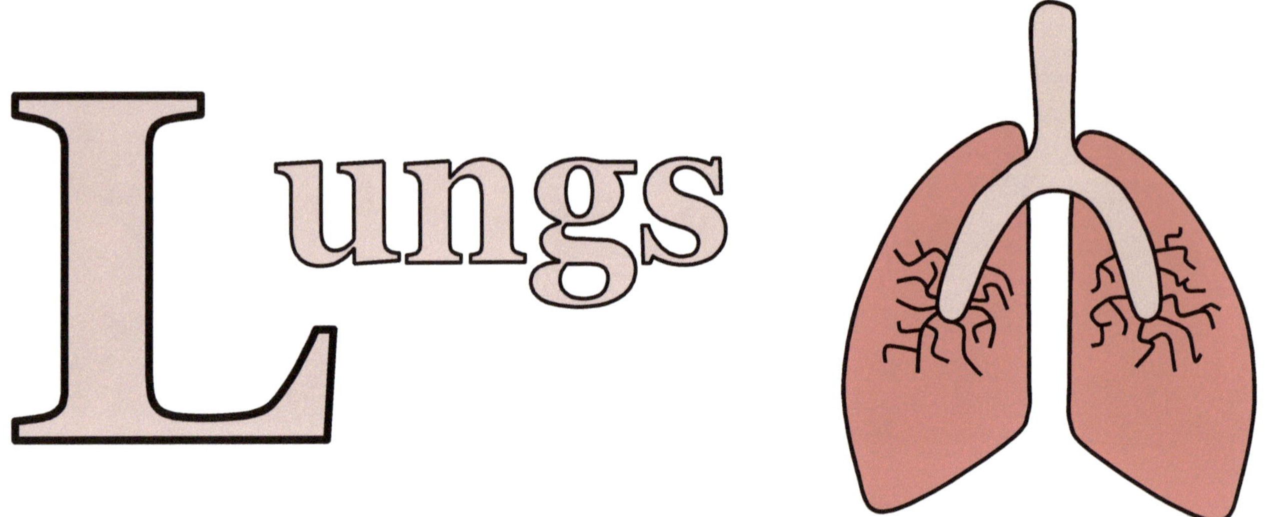

Lungs

What are lungs?

The lungs are the main organ of the respiratory system. As you inhale, oxygen travels to the lungs and travels to the lungs and exits as carbon dioxide in respiration, otherwise known as breathing.

How does blood oxygenate?

Poorly oxygenated blood enters the heart to be distributed into the lungs via the pulmonary arteries. When inhalation occurs, the deoxygenated blood becomes oxygenated and proceeds to travel back to the heart and then to the rest of the body.

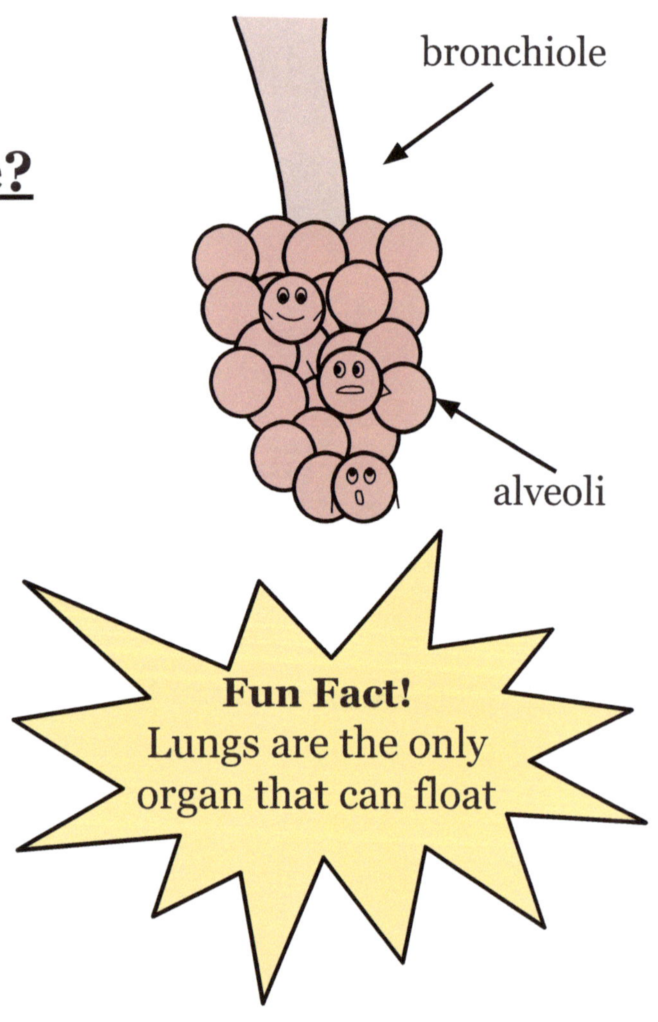

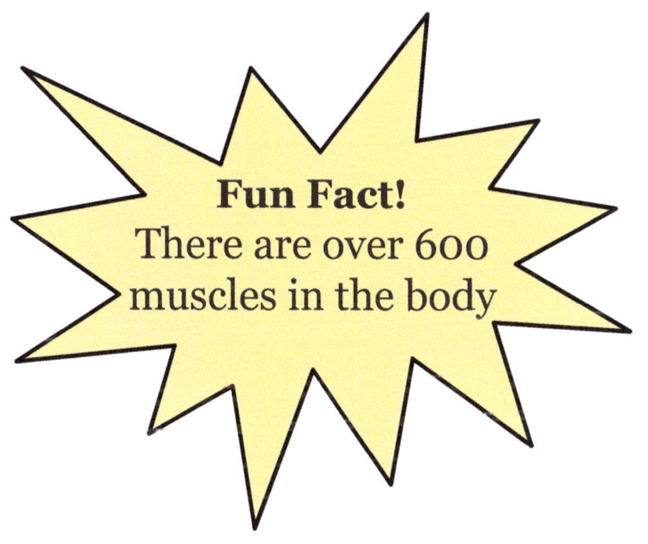

What are muscles?

Muscles are soft tissue and stretchy fibers that compose the body's muscular system. They are used for virtually everything like walking, talking, writing, chewing, and even blinking

What are the three types?

The three types of muscles are skeletal, smooth, and cardiac. Skeletal muscles are voluntary muscles that enable you to perform movements of choice such as walking. Smooth muscles are involuntary muscles that line the walls of hollow organs. Cardiac muscle is, again, an involuntary muscle that controls the heart and is only found there.

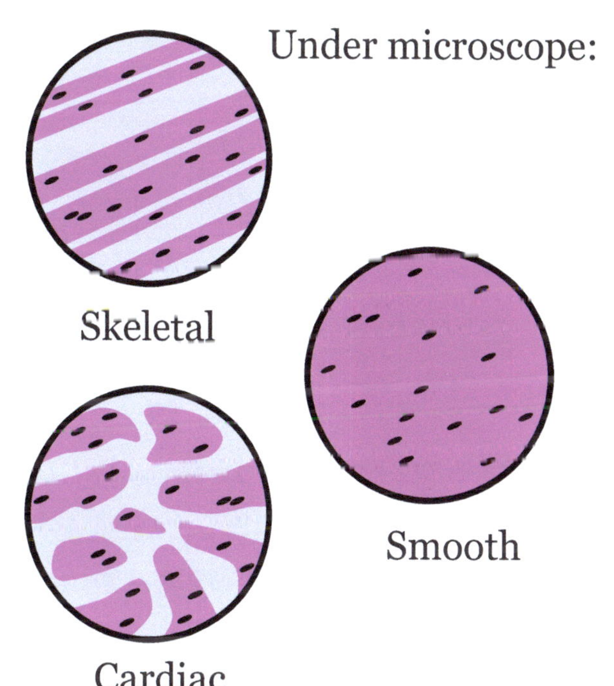

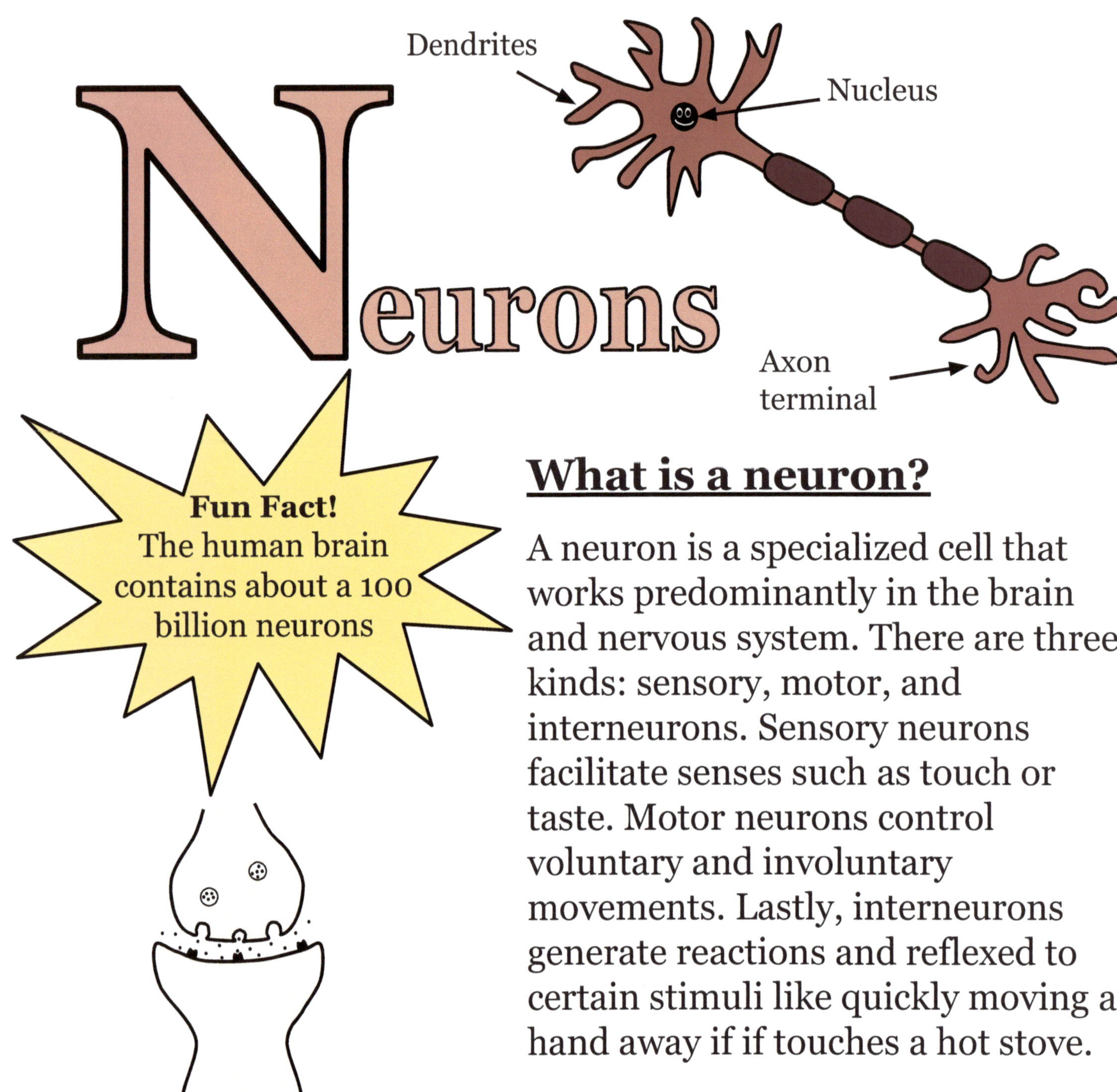Neurons

What is a neuron?

A neuron is a specialized cell that works predominantly in the brain and nervous system. There are three kinds: sensory, motor, and interneurons. Sensory neurons facilitate senses such as touch or taste. Motor neurons control voluntary and involuntary movements. Lastly, interneurons generate reactions and reflexed to certain stimuli like quickly moving a hand away if if touches a hot stove.

How do neurons communicate?

Neurons pass the message via axon terminal (which are at the end of the neuron). There can be a chemical message, which would be a neurotransmitter, or an electric signal. The dendrites (start of the neuron) receive it. The junction at where the bud and dendrite meet is called the synapse.

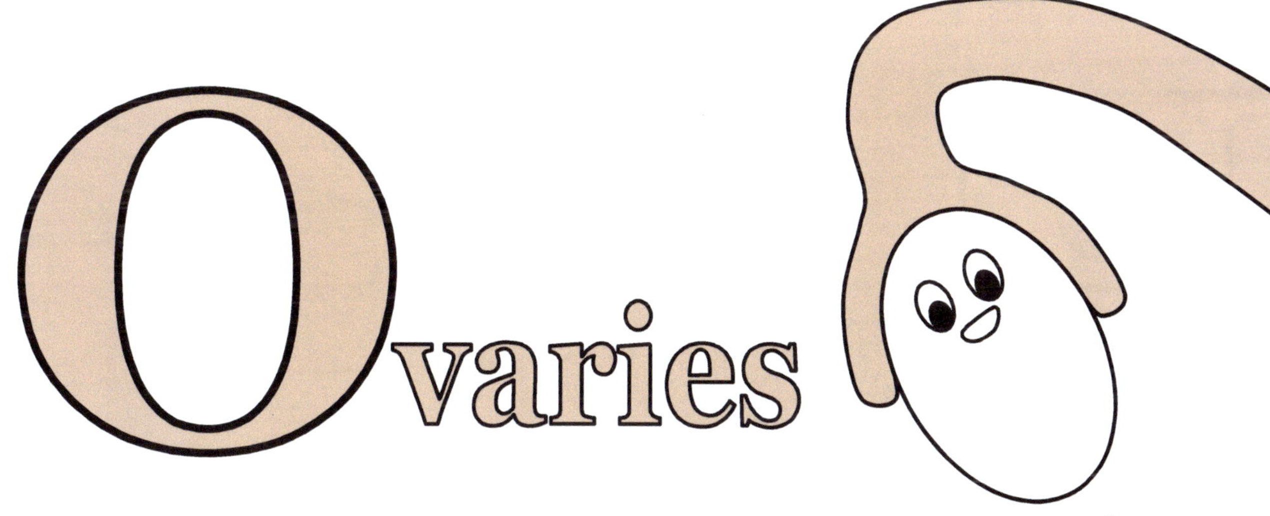 Ovaries

What are ovaries?

Ovaries are a part of a uterus found only in biological women that release hormones controlling pregnancy and menstrual cycles. Most importantly they store eggs (ovum) as well as make them for when they become fertilized and leads to a pregnancy.

What is ovulation?

Ovulation is a process where as egg stored in the ovary is released and travels through the fallopian tube and becomes subject to fertilization.

Pancreas

What is the pancreas?

The pancreas is an organ found in the abdomen under the liver that turns our food into fuel. The pancreas performs two main roles: the exocrine and endocrine function. The exocrine function focuses on digestion while the exocrine focuses on blood sugar regulation.

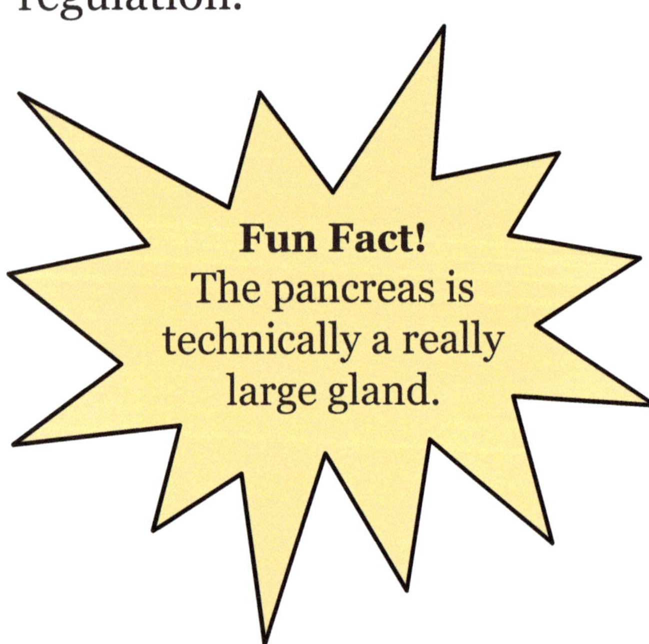

How does diabetes relate to this?

Diabetes is a disease that is the result of the pancreas being unable to convert food into fuel properly. The pancreas produces a hormone called insulin. Type 1 diabetes means the pancreas is damaged and cannot produce insulin. Type 2 diabetes occurs when the body develops a resistance to the insulin

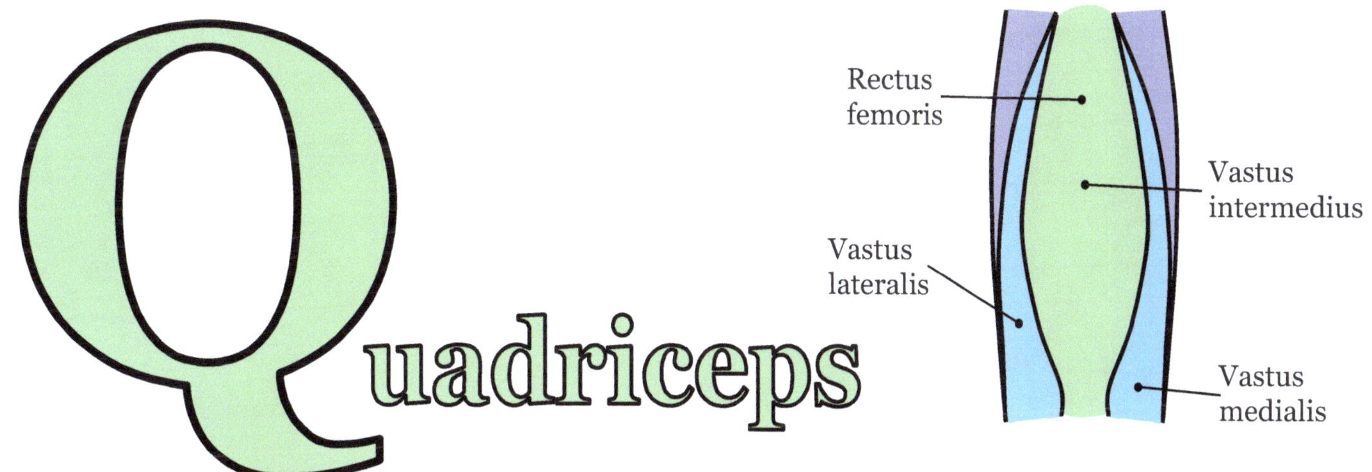uadriceps

What are quadriceps?

Quadriceps are one of the largest muscle groups in the body. They are the thigh muscles. It is made up of four different muscles: rectus femoris, vastus lateralis, vastus medialis, and vastus intermedius.

What do they do?

The quadricep muscles all work together to allow the knee to straighten or extent. They support bones such as the hip and kneecap to assure smooth functioning. Quadriceps are very important to physical activity such as walking, running, biking, etc.

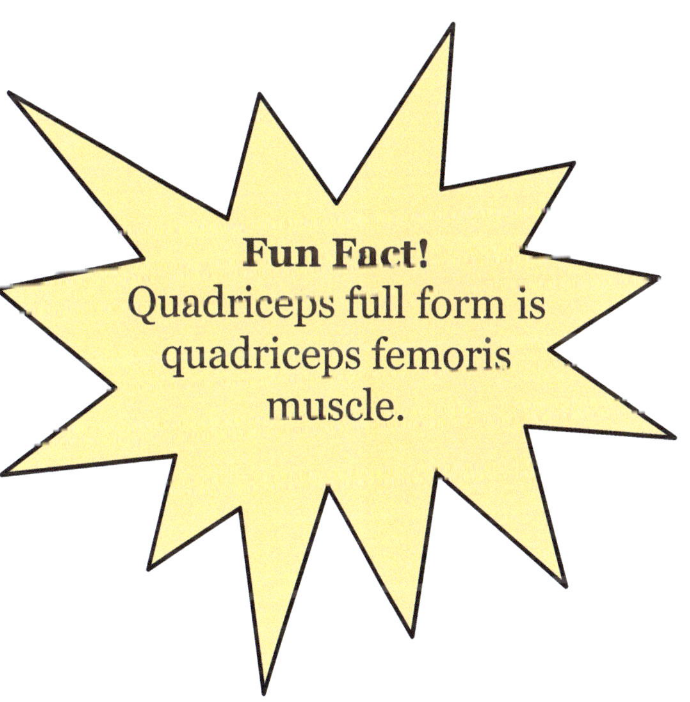

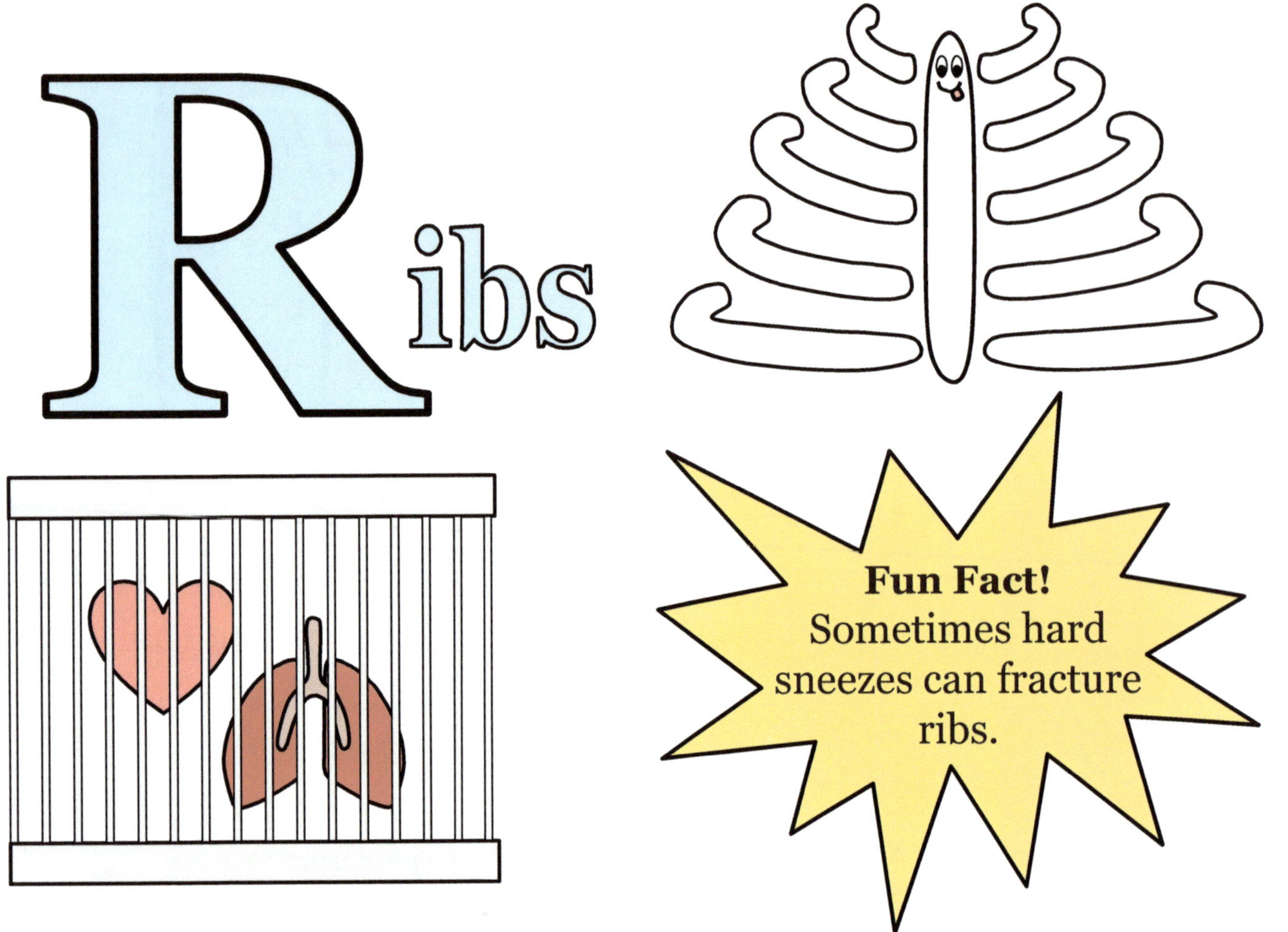

R ibs

What are ribs?

The ribs are the protective cage-like bones that expand around the thoracic organs such as the lungs and the heart. However, they mainly assist with respiration and allowing the chest to expand.

What are the different types?

In total, the average person has 12 pairs of ribs, or 24 total ribs. Of that, there are three kinds: true ribs (vertebrosternal), false ribs (vertebrochondral), and floating ribs (vertebral). 14 ribs are true, 6 ribs are false, and 4 are floating

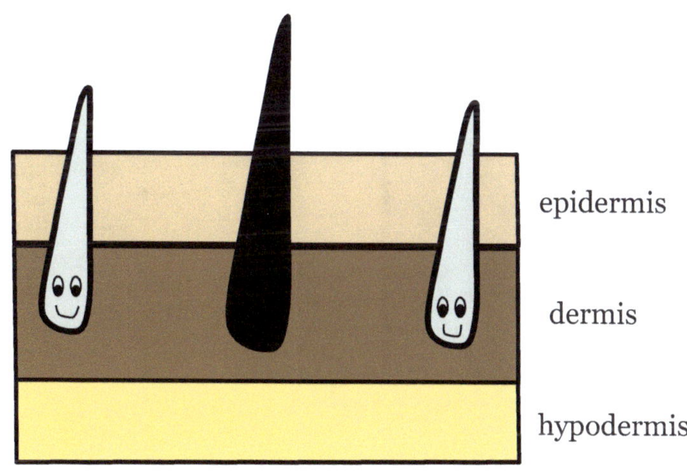

What is skin?

The skin is an organ that is the outermost and most superficial layer of the body. There are three layers that make up skin: epidermis, dermis, and hypodermis. Skin produces cells called melanocytes which produce a pigment called melanin which is the visible skin color.

What does skin do?

Firstly, the skin acts like a barrier to prevent unwanted and harmful substances/bacteria from entering the body. It also protects the body's water, fat, and nutrient amount. Also, the skin is a sensory organ so it facilitates the sense of touch as well as facilitating body temperature.

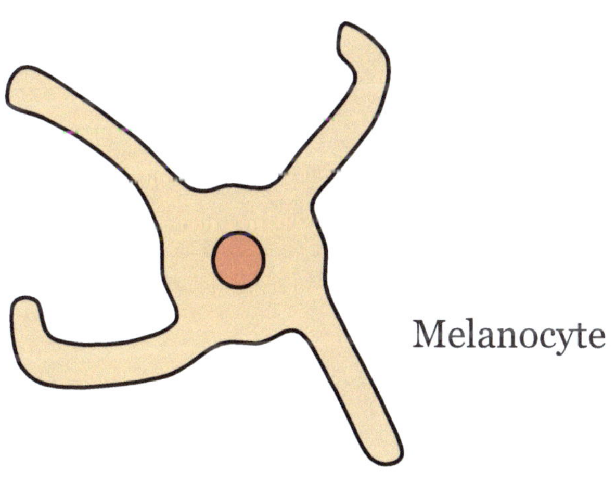

Melanocyte

Teeth

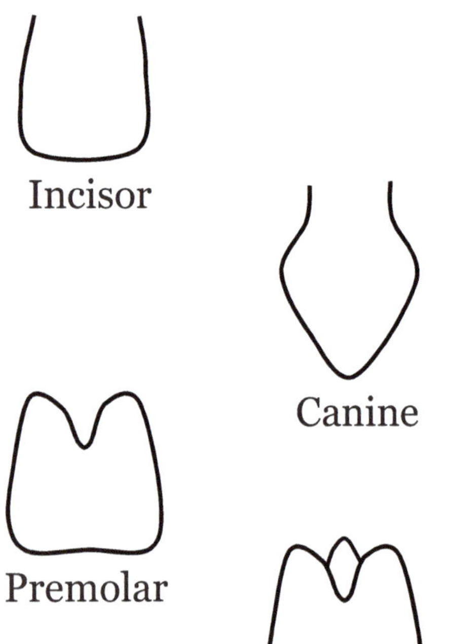

What are teeth?

In addition to being the hardest substance found in the body, teeth are incredible important for chewing, talking, and showing of a beautiful smile. Children have 20 teeth while adults typically have 32

What are the types of teeth?

Humans have four types of teeth: canines, incisors, premolars, and, molars. Canines allow for the tearing of tough foods such as different meats. Incisors allow us to bite into foods such as pizza. Premolars and molars assist with crushing foods like spinach. In a full set of adult teeth, there are 4 canines, 8 incisors, 8 premolars, amd 12 molars.

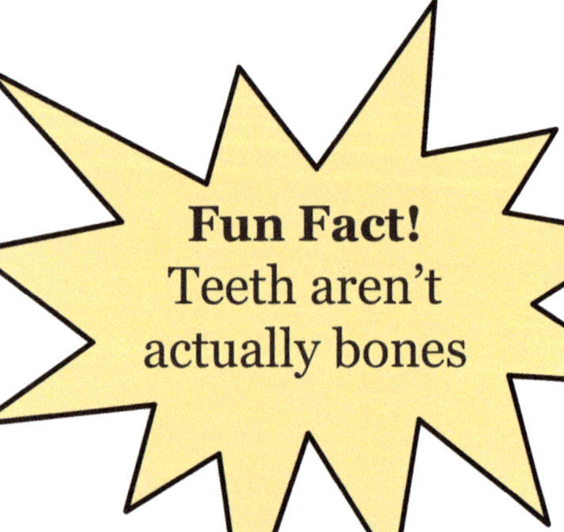

U vula

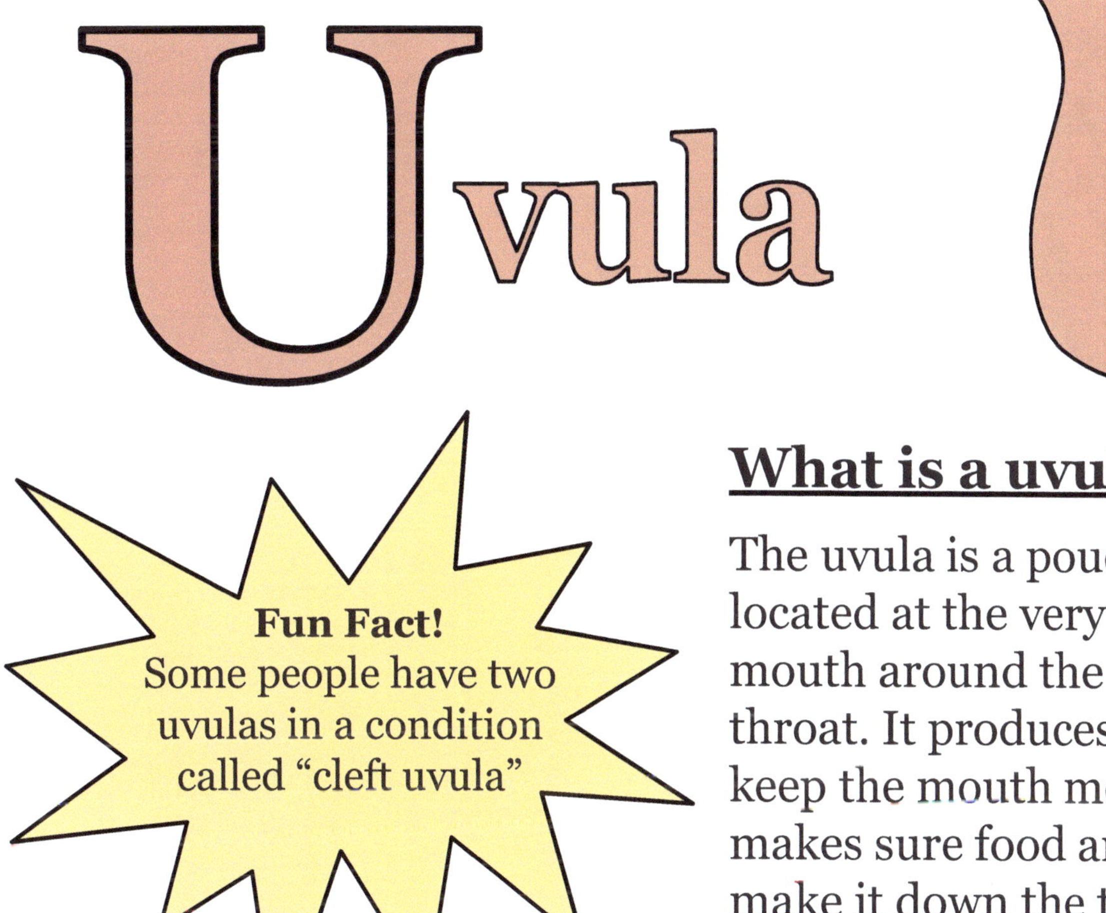

What is a uvula?

The uvula is a pouch of flesh located at the very back of the mouth around the top of the throat. It produces saliva to keep the mouth moist but also makes sure food and liquid make it down the throat and not up the nose.

What happens without one?

There are both good and bad side effects to not having a uvula. Breathing and sleeping is much easier without the obstruction especially if snoring or sleep apnea is a problem. However, it may cause a drier mouth and throat making it hard to swallow. Speech may also be affected.

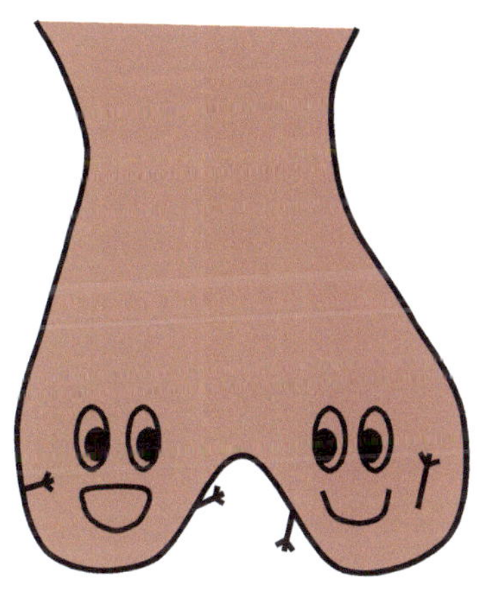

Cleft uvula

Veins

What are veins?

Veins are blood vessels that work in complete opposition to arteries. They bring deoxygenated blood from the body to the right side of the heart. After exiting the lungs post-oxygenation, the pulmonary veins will transfer the blood to the left side of the heart

Are some veins actually blue?

No! It is actually just an illusion. Veins have no real color. The light being reflected off and perceived by our eyes is blue but all of our veins appear to be red because of blood.

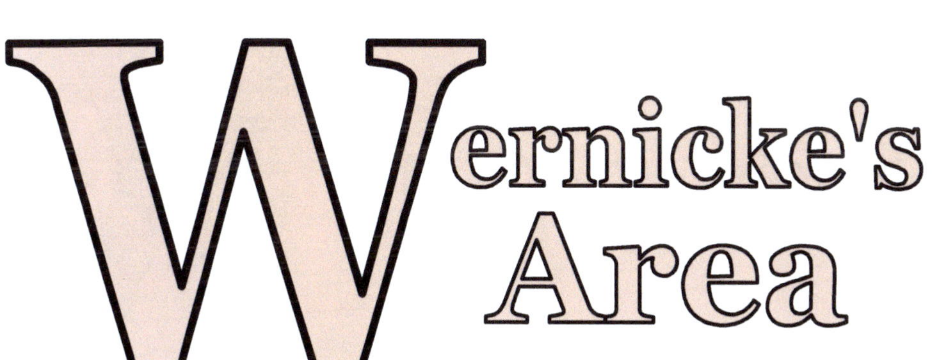

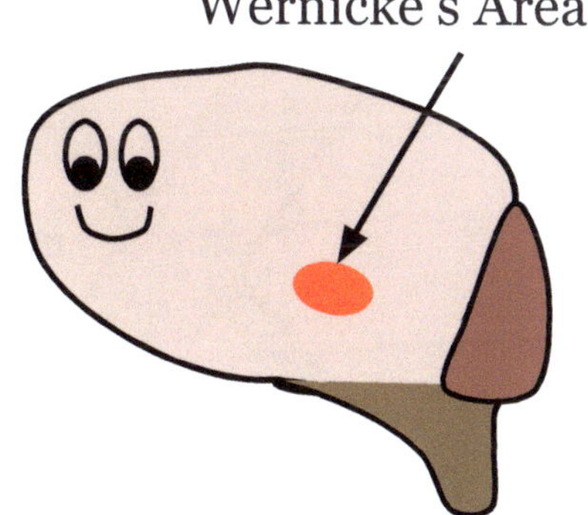

What is Wernicke's Area?

Wernicke's area is the part of the brain that is responsible for speech and comprehension. It is located towards the back of the temporal lobe in the brain. The way that Wernicke's area can comprehend speech by using motor neurons found in that brain region

What is Wernicke's pair?

A part of the brain that works in close relation to Wernicke's area in terms of function in Broca's area. While Wernicke's area deals with comprehension, Broca's area is responsible for speaking the comprehended language.

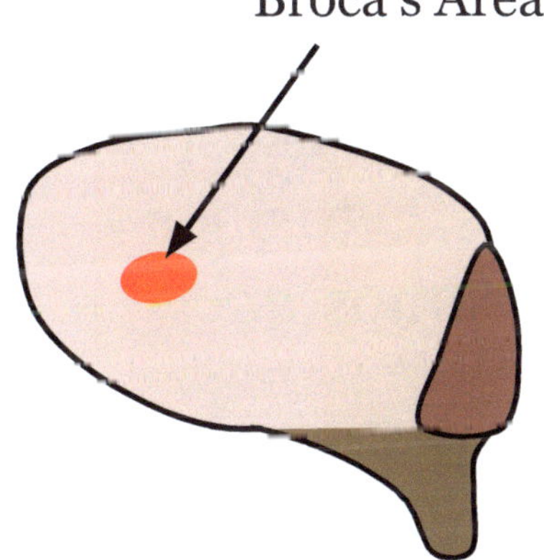

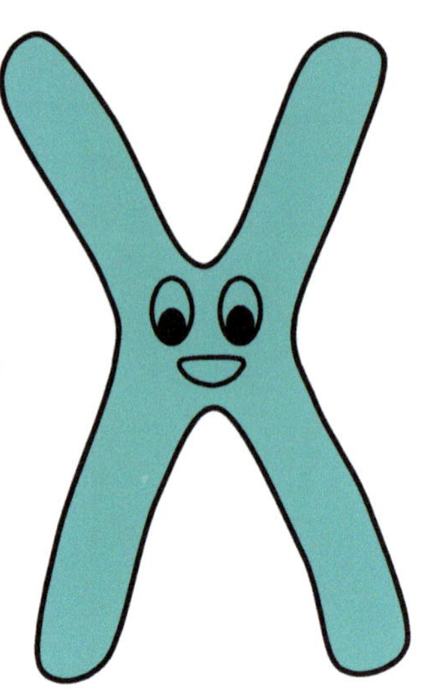

X-chromosome

What is an x-chromosome?

The x-chromosome is one of the two possible sex determining chromosomes in humans and most other animals. Only x-chromosomes are found in females as their chromosomal pair is "XX"

What are they made of?

X-chromosomes are made of DNA are made of DNA like all other chromosomes. There are approximately 155 million bases pairs (adenine, guanine, cytosine, thymine) in each x-chromosome

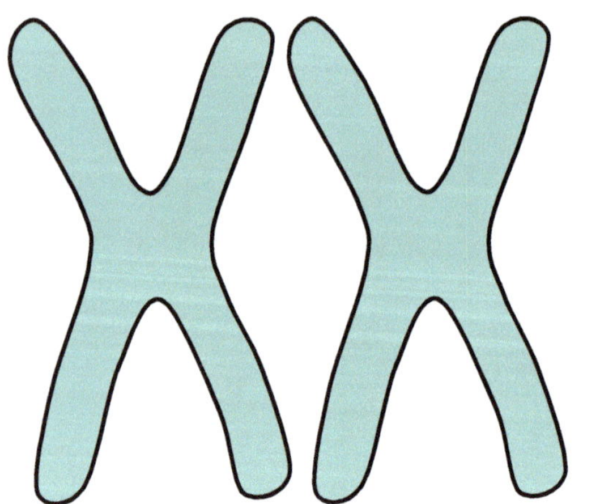

Y-chromosome

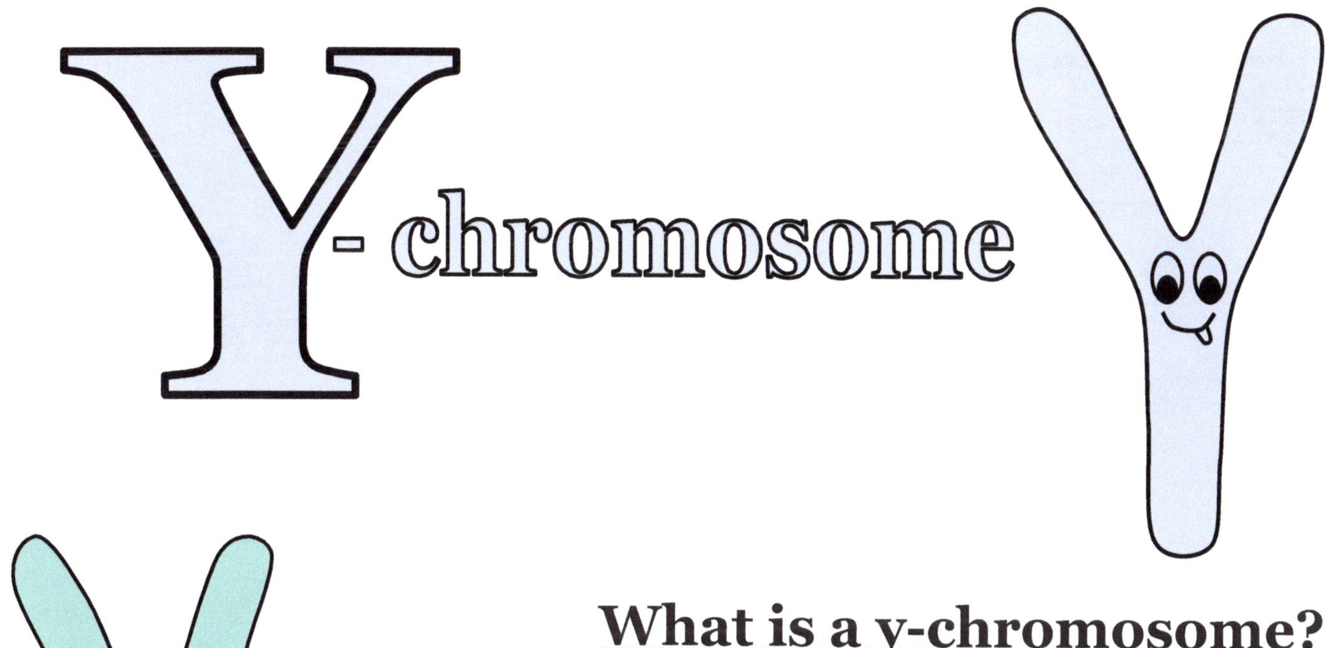

What is a y-chromosome?

The y-chromosome is the other of the two sex determining chromosomes. While it is possible to have "XX" chromosome pairs, it is impossible to have a "YY" chromosome pair

What is a y-chromosome?

Having the "XY" chromosome pair means that the recipients of the y-chromosome is biologically a male. Only the father of a child is able to determine the gender as they pass either an x or y-chromosome (not a conscious choice) to match with the mother's X-chromosome .

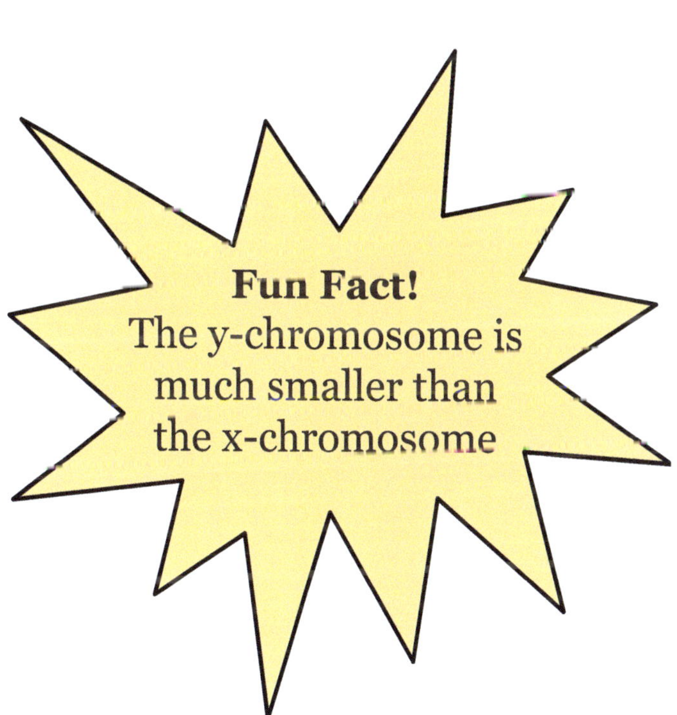

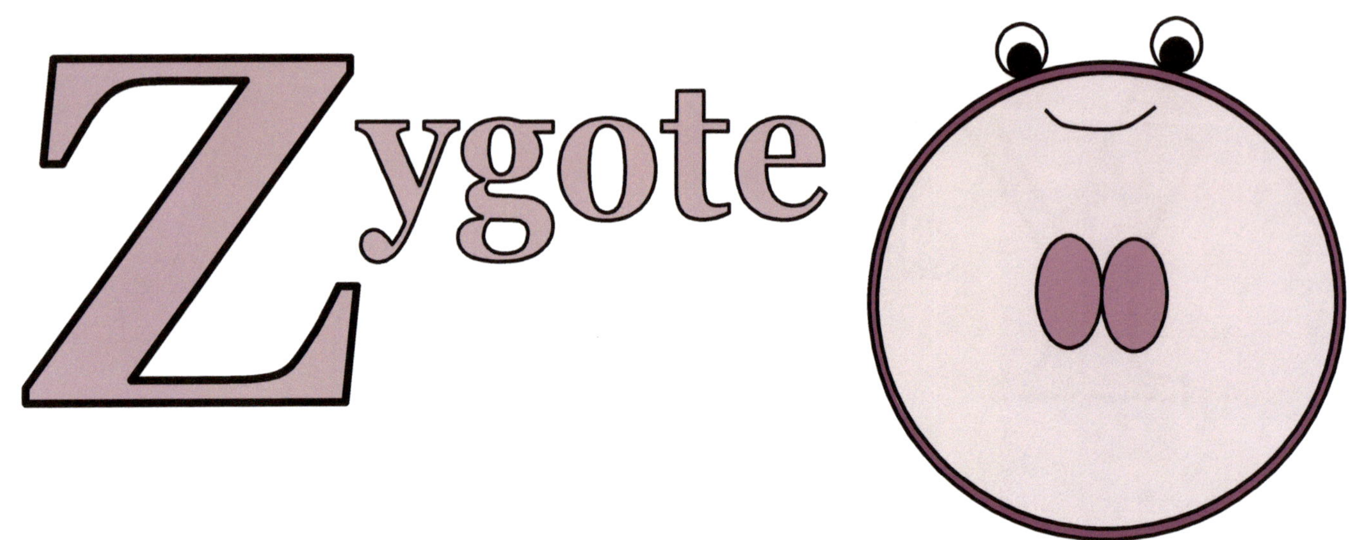Zygote

What is a zygote?

A zygote is the fertilized ovum that results from the two gametes (male's sperm and woman's egg) joining. This occurs upon conception making it the earliest stage in the development of a child

What kind of cell is a zygote?

A zygote is a diploid cell. This means that is holds two chromosome sets. One set is from the mother and the other is from the father. The alternate is a haploid cell which is just one set of chromosomes such as an individual sperm or egg.

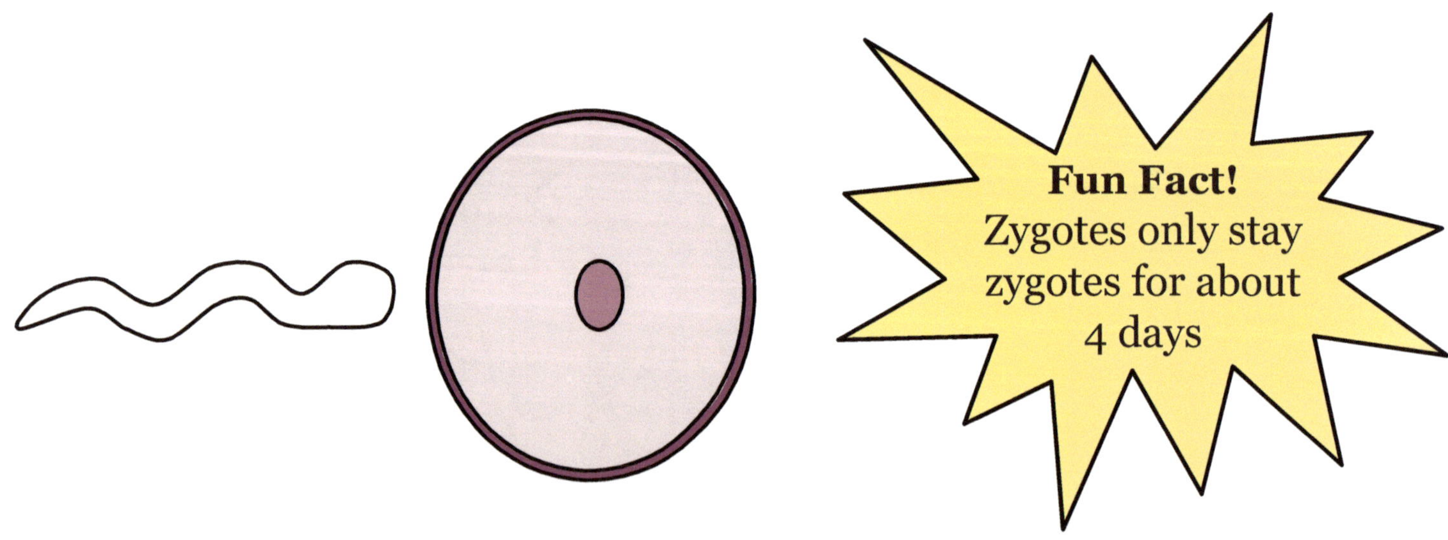